ABOLITIONISTS

What We Need Is Action

Torrey Maloof

Consultants

Vanessa Ann Gunther, Ph.D.
Department of History
Chapman University

Nicholas Baker, Ed.D.
Supervisor of Curriculum and Instruction
Colonial School District, DE

Katie Blomquist, Ed.S.
Fairfax County Public Schools

Publishing Credits

Rachelle Cracchiolo, M.S.Ed., *Publisher*
Conni Medina, M.A.Ed., *Managing Editor*
Emily R. Smith, M.A.Ed., *Series Developer*
Diana Kenney, M.A.Ed., NBCT, *Content Director*
Courtney Patterson, *Senior Graphic Designer*
Lynette Ordoñez, *Editor*

Image Credits: Cover and pp. 8 (left), 12, 17 (top), 19 (center), 22, 29 North Wind Picture Archives; cover and pp. 1, 11, 24 Bettmann/Getty Images; p. 4 NARA [528979]; p. 5 (top) LOC [LC-USZC4-544], (bottom) Sally K. Green www.sallykgreen.com; p. 6 De Agostini Picture Library/G. Dagli Orti/Bridgeman; pp. 7 (top), back cover Hulton Archive/Getty Images; p. 7 (bottom) Photo12/UIG via Getty Images; p. 8 (right) Universal History Archive/UIG/Bridgeman Images; p. 9 (bottom) LOC [LC-USZ62-112670]; pp. 9 (top left), 32 Anti-Slavery Mass Meeting Broadside, 1859 December 8. Gov. Wise Executive Papers, Library of Virginia; p. 10 (top) LOC [LC-USZ62-27876], (bottom) Stock Montage/Getty Images; p. 11 Massachussetts Historical Society; p. 13 (middle left) Napoleon Sarony Picture History/Newscom, (bottom) Sarin Images/Granger, NYC; p. 14 Serial and Government Publications Division, Library of Congress; p. 15 Hulton Archive/Getty Images; p. 17 (right) Schlesinger Library, Radcliffe Institute, Harvard University/Bridgeman Images; p. 18 (middle) Photo Researchers/Getty Images, (right) Stock Montage/Getty Images; p. 19 (left) Public Domain; pp. 20 (left), 31 National Portrait Gallery, Smithsonian Institution; p. 20 (right) Record Group 128; Records of Joint Committees of Congress, 1789-1989; National Archives; p. 21 (top) Wikimedia Commons/Public Domain, (bottom) Ken Welsh/Bridgeman Images; p. 23 Everett Collection Historical/Alamy Stock Photo; p. 23 LOC [LC-USZ62-5092]; p. 25 LOC [LC-DIG-pga-01888]; p. 26 LOC [LC-USZ62-127754]; p. 27 General Records of the United States Government; Record Group 11; National Archives; p. 29 National Geographic Creative/Alamy Stock Photo; all other images from iStock and/or Shutterstock.

Library of Congress Cataloging-in-Publication Data

Names: Maloof, Torrey, author.
Title: Abolitionists : what we need is action / Torrey Maloof.
Description: Huntington Beach, CA : Teacher Created Materials, 2017. | Includes index.
Identifiers: LCCN 2016034146 (print) | LCCN 2016044485 (ebook) | ISBN 9781493838011 (pbk.) | ISBN 9781480757660 (eBook)
Subjects: LCSH: Abolitionists--United States--History--19th century--Juvenile literature. | Antislavery movements--United States--History--19th century--Juvenile literature. | Slaves--Emancipation--United States--Juvenile literature. | African Americans--History--To 1863--Juvenile literature.
Classification: LCC E449 .M24 2017 (print) | LCC E449 (ebook) | DDC 973.7/114--dc23
LC record available at https://lccn.loc.gov/2016034146

Teacher Created Materials

5301 Oceanus Drive
Huntington Beach, CA 92649-1030
http://www.tcmpub.com

ISBN 978-1-4938-3801-1

Table of Contents

Anything to Be Free

"You have a very attentive boy, sir; but you had better watch him like a hawk when you get to the North," said the steamboat captain. He went on to warn the old white man about the "cut-throat **abolitionists**" who would try to lure his slave away from him. They would encourage him to run away and seek freedom. Little did the captain know that the old white man he was talking to was in fact an enslaved woman on her way to freedom and her "attentive boy" was her husband.

Ellen and William Craft had been enslaved in Macon, Georgia. The married couple wanted to have children but was too scared to do so. They had both been torn from their families when they were younger and could not bear the thought of their own children being taken from them. So, they devised a plan. Ellen had very light skin, and with the right disguise, they believed she could pass for an older white gentleman. William would act as her slave for the journey. The daring plan worked! They left on December 21, 1848. After traveling by ship and train, they arrived in Philadelphia on Christmas Day.
They were free!

steamboat in the 1800s

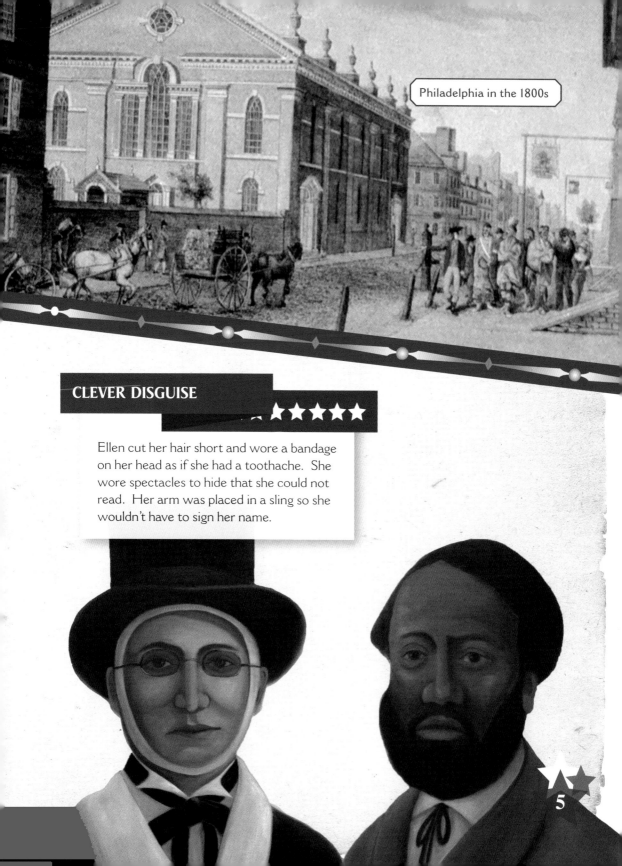

Philadelphia in the 1800s

CLEVER DISGUISE

★★★★★

Ellen cut her hair short and wore a bandage on her head as if she had a toothache. She wore spectacles to hide that she could not read. Her arm was placed in a sling so she wouldn't have to sign her name.

The Chains of Slavery

Slavery in the United States began in the early 1600s. Slave traders kidnapped Africans from their homes and forced them onto overcrowded slave ships. Conditions on these ships were horrific. People were often kept below deck. This meant no fresh air or light. They were chained with shackles and cuffs. Slave traders gave them very little food or water. Many people died during the grueling journey. Those who survived were sold at a slave auction upon their arrival in the United States.

Enslaved people in the United States endured hard labor and beatings from their masters. Even the people who had gentler masters were still stripped of their freedoms. They had no rights or liberties of any kind. They were not paid for their work. It was against the law for them to learn how to read or write. They were simply viewed as property. And as property, their owners could do whatever they liked to them.

A slave ship heads to the United States.

A slave ship arrives in Virginia in 1619.

    With the passage of the U.S. Constitution in 1788, some people began to question the **institution** of slavery. How could a country built on freedom and liberty enslave humans? Didn't the Declaration of Independence state that "all men are created equal"?

A SMALL STEP

In 1808, the United States no longer allowed newly enslaved people to be brought into the country. However, enslaved people could still be bought and sold in the United States. The price of enslaved people increased as a result.

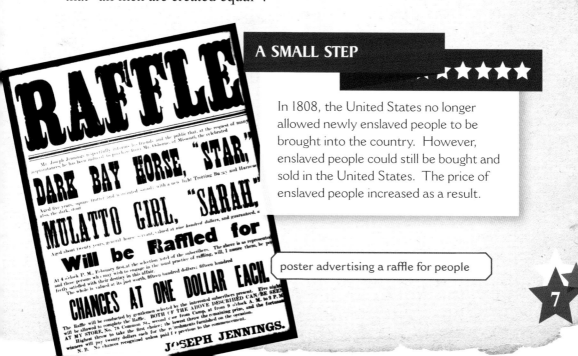

poster advertising a raffle for people

The Abolitionist Movement

The United States began as 13 colonies. After the American Revolution, it became one united nation. Yet, the states in the nation were quite different. Life in the Southern states was not the same as life in the Northern states.

In the South, the **economy** was based on farming. Most people had small farms. But some owned large farms called **plantations**. Plantation owners relied on slave labor. Enslaved people planted and picked the crops, mainly cotton. They also worked in the houses of the plantation owners. By not having to pay all these workers, the owners were able to make large profits.

PLANTATION LIFE ★★★★

An overseer controlled enslaved people working on plantations. If enslaved people weren't working fast enough, made mistakes, or even looked at an overseer in a way he didn't like, they could be whipped or beaten.

In the North, factories were the norm. The North was more industrial. Its economy was built on **manufacturing**. People in the North made, sold, and transported goods. Factories had workers, but they were paid. Although the North used slave labor in its early days, it slowly **abolished** it over the years. By the 1830s, many people in the North saw slavery as an evil institution. They wanted to abolish it throughout the country. They began to create organizations and antislavery societies. The abolitionist movement had begun.

Police break up an abolitionist meeting in Boston in 1860.

ANTI-SLAVERY MASS MEETING!

Agreeably to a call, signed by about 50 persons, and published in the Lawrence Republican, a Mass Meeting of the friends of Freedom will be held at Miller's Hall, at 2 o'clock P. M., on Friday, Dec. 2d, the day on which

CAPT. JOHN BROWN IS TO BE EXECUTED, To testify against the iniquitous SLAVE POWER that rules this Nation, and take steps to

Organize the Anti-Slavery Sentiment of the community. Arrangements have been made with prominent speakers to be present and address the meeting.
PER ORDER OF COMMITTEE OF ARRANGEMENTS.
Lawrence, Nov. 26, 1859.

The Main Players

One of the pioneers of the abolitionist movement was a man named William Lloyd Garrison. Garrison grew up in Massachusetts. He was raised with strong Christian **values**. As an adult, he opposed slavery. He called for its immediate end. He wanted all slaves to be freed at once.

William Lloyd Garrison

In 1829, Garrison wrote an article. In it, he called a ship owner and a ship captain "highway robbers and murderers." They were transporting enslaved people from the North to the South. The men sued Garrison. He was found guilty of **libel**. The judge ordered him to pay $100, or spend six months in jail. Garrison couldn't pay the fine, so he opted for jail time. While in jail, he wrote antislavery letters and sent them to newspaper editors. It was not long before Garrison's name was well known across the nation.

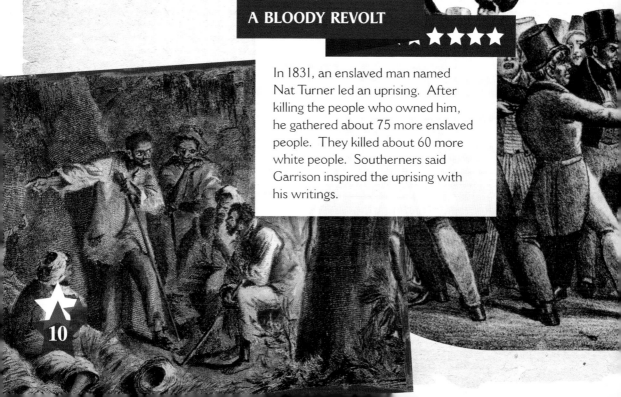

A BLOODY REVOLT ★★★★

In 1831, an enslaved man named Nat Turner led an uprising. After killing the people who owned him, he gathered about 75 more enslaved people. They killed about 60 more white people. Southerners said Garrison inspired the uprising with his writings.

After he was released from jail, Garrison started making speeches for antislavery groups. He met with formerly enslaved people. He listened to their horrific stories. He was now more determined than ever to abolish slavery. In 1831, Garrison started his own antislavery newspaper. It was called the *Liberator*. In the first edition he wrote, "I will be heard." And he was.

1865 issue of the *Liberator*

This 1835 political cartoon of an abolitionist meeting features Garrison being robbed and pulled through the streets.

Men were not the only people fighting for abolition. Nor were all abolitionists from the North. Two sisters in South Carolina were also fighting to make a difference. Sarah and Angelina Grimké grew up on a large plantation. Their family enslaved many people. Yet, the two sisters were never comfortable with slavery. They felt in their hearts that it was wrong. They could not stand the sight of people being beaten and abused by their own family members.

In 1819, Sarah took her ailing father to Philadelphia for treatment. It was there that she met a religious group called the Society of Friends. Its members were called **Quakers**. They were against violence and slavery. Sarah felt at home with the Quakers. She and her sister later moved to Philadelphia and became Quakers. The two women started speaking out against slavery.

Sarah Grimké

Angela Grimké

Southerners were outraged and shocked by the sisters' actions. But the sisters **persevered**. They gave speeches and wrote letters and **pamphlets** against slavery. This angered the Northerners and the Quakers, too. Women were not supposed to write or speak about such a controversial topic. But the sisters did not let that stop them. They dedicated their lives to the antislavery movement.

JOINING A SECOND FIGHT

The Grimké sisters also joined the Women's Suffrage Movement. This movement sought to give voting rights to women. Many people who supported the movement were also abolitionists. The sisters became close friends with one of the movement's leaders, Elizabeth Cady Stanton (right).

Quaker meetinghouse

Perhaps the most famous abolitionist at this time was a man named Frederick Douglass. Douglass was an enslaved man who had escaped to freedom. He started a new life in Massachusetts. Every week, Douglass bought Garrison's antislavery newspaper the *Liberator*. In 1841, the two men met. This meeting changed Douglass's life.

Garrison felt Douglass's life story could be a powerful tool. He believed that if others heard the story, it would help them understand that slaves were people, not property. They had feelings. They had hopes and dreams. Garrison felt that Douglass could also make people realize the horrors of slavery. He wanted people to know how enslaved people were really treated in the South. He asked Douglass to share his story at an antislavery meeting.

THE NORTH STAR

Douglass also started his own newspaper called the *North Star*. It was a fitting title. People escaping slavery used the North Star to guide them to freedom.

At first, Douglass was nervous. He did not think he had the courage to speak in front of a large crowd. But, he refused to give in to fear. He spoke to the crowd, and he was a natural. Douglass was a commanding **orator**. His honest and moving words inspired people to join the abolitionists' cause.

Douglass continued to give speeches. One day, the Massachusetts Anti-Slavery Society offered him a job. They paid him to travel and share his story. Before long, he was one of the most popular speakers in the country.

FREE AT LAST ★★★★

Douglass worried that his old master would find him and force him back into slavery. So, Douglass traveled to England, where slavery was illegal. Abolitionists there paid his former master for his freedom. Douglass was now a truly free man.

Frederick Douglass

15

The Underground Railroad

Abolitionists gave speeches and wrote articles. They published pamphlets and authored books. But one of their most powerful weapons was the Underground Railroad. This secret network of safe houses helped enslaved people travel to the North where they could be free.

The Underground Railroad was made of various routes. Along these routes were "stations." These were safe places where people could rest. Sometimes, they could get food or clean clothing at a station. A station might be a Quaker meetinghouse or an attic of an abolitionist's home. Enslaved people were called "passengers" or "cargo." And "conductors" were people who guided the passengers from station to station. These code words helped keep the system a secret.

A DANGEROUS JOURNEY

★★★★★

Passengers had to be extremely cautious. If they were caught, they could be sent back to their masters or killed. To be safe, many people traveled at night and hid during the day.

Abolitionist William Still is often referred to as the Father of the Underground Railroad. He was the director of multiple stations. He also risked his life as a conductor. It is said that he helped almost 800 enslaved people escape.

Harriet Tubman was also a conductor. She was as tough as nails. After making her own daring journey to freedom, Tubman returned to the South multiple times to help her family and friends escape. But she did not stop there. For 10 years, she bravely led nearly 300 people to freedom.

William Still

Harriet Tubman

The Path to War

The 1850s was a turbulent time in the United States. The issue of slavery threatened to tear the nation apart. The Compromise of 1850 heightened the tension. It was a series of five laws passed by Congress. One law admitted California to the **Union** as a free state. Slavery was not permitted. A second law admitted New Mexico and Utah, too. Each of these states would make its own decision to be a free state or a slave state. The Texas border was adjusted as part of the third law. The fourth law made the slave trade illegal in Washington, DC. This made abolitionists happy. But, the fifth law outraged them. This was the Fugitive Slave Act.

Congress meets to discuss the Compromise of 1850.

A POWERFUL STORY

★★★★★

The passage of the Fugitive Slave Act inspired Harriet Beecher Stowe (right) to publish *Uncle Tom's Cabin*. Her story illustrated the violence and struggle of slavery. The first year the book was published, it sold 1.5 million copies!

18

The Fugitive Slave Act stated that runaway slaves must be returned to their masters. All citizens were required to help return runaway slaves. This had been a law for some time, but the new version was even harsher. Anyone who helped enslaved people escape would now be subjected to large fines or even jail time. It also denied fugitive slaves the right to a trial by jury. Formerly enslaved people who were living free in the North were now scared. They could be captured at any time and sent to the South. Many left the North and moved to Canada where slavery was illegal.

A man tries to escape slavery.

19

Some abolitionists were getting impatient. They felt more needed to be done than just giving speeches and writing pamphlets. They called for an immediate abolition of slavery no matter the cost. "What we need is action!" declared John Brown. Brown was a **radical** abolitionist. He felt that a war was needed to end slavery.

In 1854, a new act created a violent uproar. The Kansas-Nebraska Act ended the Missouri Compromise. Under the old compromise, Kansas and Nebraska should have been added to the Union as free states. But, this new act said that these states could choose to be slave states or free states. The North was furious, and so was John Brown!

People poured into Kansas and Nebraska. Proslavery groups and abolitionists fought to gain control of the territories. Violent fights broke out between the two sides. This period of time became known as Bleeding Kansas. Brown formed a **militia** (mi-LISH-uh) with his sons and headed to Kansas. While there, they attacked and killed five proslavery men who had burned down a town. This would not be Brown's last act of violence in the name of abolition.

MISSOURI COMPROMISE

In 1820, Missouri became a slave state, while Maine was added as a free state. This kept the number of free and slave states in the country balanced. The compromise also stated that future states north of Missouri's southern border would be free.

John Brown

the Missouri Compromise

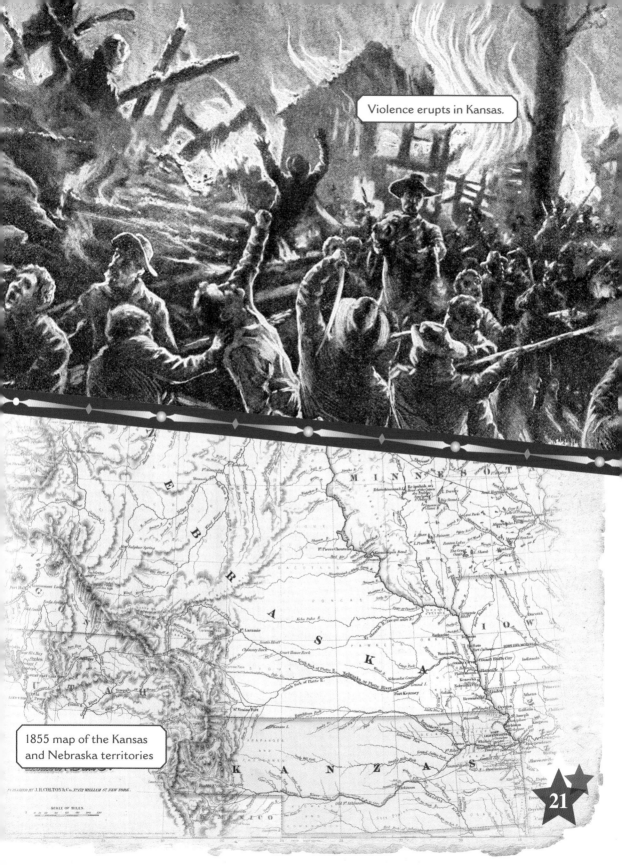

Violence erupts in Kansas.

1855 map of the Kansas and Nebraska territories

In 1857, Brown started formulating a plan. He began recruiting fighters and raising funds. Later, Brown rented a farm in Maryland near Harpers Ferry. That town housed a **federal arsenal**. Brown planned to raid the arsenal and take all the weapons. The weapons would be given to enslaved people so they could rise up against their masters. The plan was dangerous. Even Frederick Douglass warned Brown not to go through with it. But, his mind was made up.

On October 16, 1859, Brown and his 21 men snuck into Harpers Ferry in the middle of the night. They rounded up 60 hostages and raided the arsenal and a few other places in town. Everything went according to plan until daybreak. Brown assumed enslaved people in the area would revolt. Instead, local residents saw what was happening and brought their own militias. No enslaved people revolted. Brown and his men were trapped inside the arsenal. When it was all over, 10 of Brown's men were dead. Five had escaped. The rest had been caught, including a wounded Brown. Brown was quickly brought to trial and found guilty. On December 2, 1859, he was hanged.

Soldiers capture John Brown at Harpers Ferry.

John Brown's trial

DRED SCOTT DECISION

Dred Scott was an enslaved man who sued for his freedom. In 1857, the Supreme Court ruled that he couldn't sue for freedom because enslaved people had no legal rights. This added to the mounting tension in the nation.

23

Lincoln becomes the 16th president.

24

The abolitionists took their next step toward ending slavery. They voted for Abraham Lincoln to be the next president. Although Lincoln had said he would not end slavery in the South, he did promise that he would not let it spread. People in the South did not trust him. Before Lincoln could even take office, Southern states started to **secede**. Lincoln vowed to keep the Union together, even if that meant war.

The nation had officially torn in two. In 1861, the South formed its own country called the Confederate States of America. The North became known as the Union. In April of that year, the Confederate army fired shots on Fort Sumter. The war had begun. The Civil War lasted four long years. It was the bloodiest war in American history. More than 620,000 died and many more were injured. The war ended in 1865, when the South surrendered to the Union. In December of that year, the 13th **Amendment** became law. It abolished slavery once and for all.

Union and Confederate forces battle in Pea Ridge, Arkansas.

A New Battle Begins

Slavery had been abolished, but another battle was just beginning. Millions of freed slaves now had to adjust to a new way of living. It was not an easy task. They needed jobs so that they could earn money. Many were homeless after the war. They needed food, clothing, and shelter. Abolitionists shifted their attention to helping African Americans start over. But they also had another goal. They wanted all African Americans to have equal rights and protection under the law—something that was not given to them after the war.

Although free, African Americans suffered greatly after the war. They faced harassment and violence. They were met with **racism** at every turn. **Segregation** laws separated white people from black people. This caused more hatred and division. For the next 100 years, they fought bravely for equality. They did not back down or give up their dreams. They had won their freedom. And now, they were determined to win their rights.

This 1874 illustration shows African Americans being denied the right to vote.

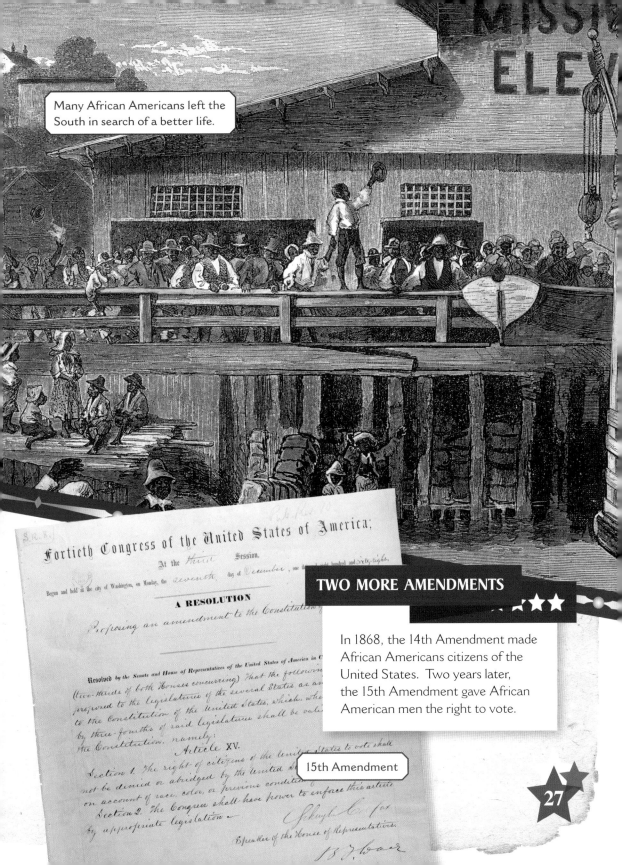

Many African Americans left the South in search of a better life.

TWO MORE AMENDMENTS ★★

In 1868, the 14th Amendment made African Americans citizens of the United States. Two years later, the 15th Amendment gave African American men the right to vote.

15th Amendment

Share It!

The Underground Railroad was not the only way enslaved people escaped to freedom. Many courageous people took matters into their own hands. They were daring and smart. They were willing to take any risks necessary to reach freedom in the North.

Conduct research using the Internet or library resources. Find one of the many amazing stories of escape. Then, share it! Tell the story in detail to your friends and family.

Glossary

abolished—to have officially ended or stopped something

abolitionists—people who were against slavery and worked to end it

amendment—a change to the words or meaning of a law or document

economy—the system of buying and selling goods and services

federal arsenal—a place where a government stores military equipment and weapons

institution—a practice or custom that is accepted by many

libel—something written or spoken that damages a person's good name

manufacturing—making raw materials into finished products

militia—regular citizens trained in military combat and willing to fight and defend their country

orator—a skillful public speaker who gives powerful speeches

pamphlets—small and short printed publications with no cover that are about a particular subject

persevered—continued doing something even in the face of great difficulty

plantations—large farms that produce crops for money

Quakers—members of a Christian religious group who dress simply, are against violence, and have meetings without a special ceremony

racism—the belief that some races of people are superior over others

radical—having extreme social or political views that are not shared by many people

secede—to formally separate from a nation or state

segregation—the practice of separating groups of people based on their race or religion

Union—term used to describe the United States of America; also the name given to the Northern army during the Civil War

values—strongly held beliefs about what is right and wrong

Index

Your Turn!

ANTI-SLAVERY MASS MEETING!

Agreeably to a call, signed by about 50 persons, and published in the Lawrence Republican, a Mass Meeting of the friends of Freedom will be held at Miller's Hall, at 2 o'clock P. M., on Friday, Dec. 2d, the day on which

CAPT. JOHN BROWN IS TO BE EXECUTED,

To testify against the iniquitous SLAVE POWER that rules this Nation, and take steps to

Organize the Anti-Slavery Sentiment

of the community. Arrangements have been made with prominent speakers to be present and address the meeting.

PER ORDER OF COMMITTEE OF ARRANGEMENTS.

Lawrence, Nov. 26, 1859.

Abolitionist Meeting

This document advertises an abolitionist meeting in Lawrence, Kansas. The meeting was scheduled for the day of John Brown's execution. The organizers hoped the event would rally support for their cause.

Create your own poster to advertise an abolitionist meeting. Include the date and time of the event. You might want to choose an important date for your meeting, too. Use persuasive language to explain why people should attend the event.